THIEVES' AFTERNOON

Rose Styron

THIEVES'
AFTERNOON

The Viking Press
New York

First published in 1973 by The Viking Press, Inc.
625 Madison Avenue, New York, N.Y. 10022

Published simultaneously in Canada by
The Macmillan Company of Canada Limited

SBN 670-70029-0

Library of Congress catalog card number: 72-9700
Printed in U.S.A.

ACKNOWLEDGMENTS

"Sonata" originally appeared in *The American Scholar*. "Cemetery: Litchfield County," and "Note in a Bottle" (under the title of "Afterward") originally appeared in *Harper's*. "A Swim at Dawn" and "Martha's Vineyard" originally appeared in *Vineyard Gazette*. "Nomen" and "Train Across America" originally appeared in *The Yale Review*.

for Bill

Contents

——————————*Islands of Childhood*——————————

Chansonnier

THIEVES' AFTERNOON [3]

Two of us barelegged,
our backs to the ocean:
thieves' afternoon
on the pier of July,

our thoughts quiet
as windows on a garden,
senses bobbing
with skiff and sky.

Time that was running out
turns in the stillness
pulls the fresh hours
out of sheer blue air

deepens by duplicate
knowledge our language:
a word for a vision,
a sigh for the long season's care. ■

The signs change.
I will change my life.
Your unjustness
is my justice,
knife for knife.

Who if I cried
would hear me
when the world rains?

Across the continent
always on pleasant trains
I played at least two
word games at a time
with him and you.

There was no need
to write things down,
scores, for instance, or rhyme
old loss and new.

Everyone understood.
And I was good.

Age, a storm,
or excess of religion or response
to cello music
and sudden jagged landscapes exploding into
beauty after the scheduled plains,
betrays the mind.

I find
constantly your eyes,
see in their darkness now only
lightning, my own dreams.

Oh if I could
I'd catch their perilous light,
their schemes
and hold them,
keep us safe tonight,
abandoning the angelic orders.

To have you see me as I was . . .
I suppose you must.
Games like poems
turn upon the news:
love is unjust.

■

Arrows:
You are hurt.
No way to touch you.
Fear
ravels the words
I came to say.

A light streaks.
You are too close,
too straight,
too still.
We're not to be alone
this thundering day.

Arrows:
Small talk.
A waste of smiles.
No love. No love.
Perfect good-byes,
witnessed as played.

Comedian of despair,
I seek
a stake, ropes,
arrows.
We are but saints,
Sebastians, self-betrayed.   ■

MIME

Losing hold
on such legends as
pure Arabian horses daring
the midnight wind together
(how high they disappear!)

I fall
to rainforest dreams:
clear waters gentler than
your cooling breath asleep
where I rose to go

(the instinct of darkness,
part man's, part fool's,
my instructor,
loving you so

precipitously)
fall
over the vertical
rock and the prisms of stones
by newborn sky-green
ferns, below.

Endlessly
my thoughts of you
precede me down
where the early pools
reflecting our conversations
surreally hide.
I need your tears.

Endlessly
my desire for you
chastens me
and the noon waters,
escaping conversation,
catch, slide.
I need your tears.

A lizard
changing his skin again
regards me.
Old sunlight
piercing the deep
green elephant-ear

cathedral reveals old
emeralds of fear,
their shimmer finds me
no matter where
I believing in you
downward
under slippery hollows
climb.

Pursue me
if you've time
or the nonsense to care.
I won't count on your coming.

Meanwhile, my mime
(I love you for your
strict gestures), make
friends with light;
the blind day follows
a waterfall's lute.

Scorn nothing. Mark
the odd vermilion orchid,
the scents of broken
coffee bean and ginger root,
wild cinnamons. Choose
the ripe vine's fruit.

Should your journey be long
as mine and steep,
learn the myriad
rainbird song.
Let the promise of caves

be forgot,
whether we somewhere
surprise ourselves or not,
for a child
in love with every dark
as you or I may lose
his way in the intricate naves

escaping the cross
of passion,
the windowing sun,
the obvious graves.

■

I dream we are in Paris
having lunch.
It's May,
the city in a blowing branch
of red quince
framed. All night
the birds fly in and out
my country window.
Sun, baring a skylight,
lasers the afternoon buffet:
peaches of Provence, pale salmon,
lemons fresh from Campania's terrace
and rougail and arugola and fancy's
rue, a marquee
for the swans of ice.

You come to sit beside me,
lightly fiddling with my hand
that tries the latch under
the quince window,
and when you smile too suddenly
your smile, tilting now, too
near, the birds light
quietly,
the sunlight
pierces my extravagant ring
and I am a child
full of brilliance, dumb.

A chance. The dream
flickers, for in this intensity
of light I mean to hold the chance
to tell you all I
dared not say
when it was growing light
and you paced in and out of the birch
woods, waiting,
an early shadow
longer than the brick-edged lawn,
an April day.

This time
as the radiance of a windy night
attracts the morning in its search
for quiet light
and the various sounds of morning,
intruders from childhood, come
and you are gone,
I shall not fly
even for the space of dreams.   ∎

Finding I loved you
I learned to lie

not to pretend
that sky was sea

or daybreak, noon
(would you have known?)

and not to deny
who you were for me

but to lie beside you
saying I loved

more than you, the world.
So near, so new

was my sense of being
(forever, I meant) there

perhaps I, shining,
persuaded you

that my whim was truth
and truth the lie

and you let me leave,
you let me be.

It doesn't matter
what I was to you

it's who you were
for me.

TO SAMARKAND

Keep my secret:
I have been to Samarkand
and back, alone,
not in our dream.

The sky bore no constellations
then, the tree no wings,
the earth no wheat,
its minstrel bent, bone.

Among a thousand travelers, alone
through Africa and Asia and strange
continents of sense,
never forgetting you, I saw

the land of Tamburlaine.
His ancient enemies were caged
and taunted on the boulevard,
their faces too familiar.

Never forgetting you, I saw,
still turquoise to the sun,
shining through centuries of brute and bard

those domes. Above them,
silver Karnai horns announced
for the mosaic of my afternoon

girls with sixteen braids apiece
to sing, old patriarchs reciting,
the sway of satin dancers, tambourines.

Here the king's wife, Bibi Hanim,
waking in the courtyard, the king away,
bore the brand of an infamous kiss,
bartered her pride for a shrine.

The tiles dazzled. The king forgave her,
but her architect was gone,
darkening the skies toward Bukhara.

Love, if you forget me
or remember
keep my secret. I wake
in Samarkand, forgiven, alone.

Melons spill all around us now,
the sky is bright with wings and a new star,
the grapes hang down,
and roses bloom and bloom. . . .   ■

SONATA

coming upon Mozart
suddenly, flute
and cello in the dark,
I am confounded
by tears
for one whose music
fills and marks
forever
a room I thought
abandoned

∎

THE WINTER PALACE

Leningrad. October.
Snowfall at dark. I stand,
courtiers arrayed behind me in frames of
far scenic attire
—Titian in Egypt, Matisse
on the lawn,
Delacroix with lions
at the hunt—
where Peter stood,
gazing out on his Palace Square.

From this high window in the Hermitage
snow melting like memory
on the uneven glass
I forge signs to the Archangel
black and brooding on his towering
column there.

Listen, my fingertips and paned
breath whisper,
I have found you.
Half a lifetime heard my walk
with Rembrandt and Bonnard, down noisy flowered
streets in Amsterdam, in Baltimore, in Vence.

Through my domain, lyric of England,
legend of Moors,
and near cathedraled landscapes I have dreamed
this Winter Palace,
green and white and gold, this
Winter Palace

caught in the glass cabinet of time
as in our breakfront
once when I was small
ancestral Rockingham like china fox-grapes
held me, green and white and gold.

What can you sing me, wild black Archangel
poised on your fearful column,
what can you hear?

The moon clanking over the fortress
Our Lady of Kazan in chains
Raskolnikov down endless cobbled
alleys, courtyards of laundry, stone-faced
stairways of Petropolis, pursued.

No lovesongs that I came for,
yours and mine?
Under the hazardous arcs of light
our lips our fingers still could touch
though all the palace trumpets
sounded and the ships sank.
Who can escape assassins, by himself?

My old friend Rembrandt
and my kin, Bonnard,
helped me to break the crystal nightlock
of the Palace, escorted me upstairs.
I am alone now, inside
brimming against the runny glass.

Beyond the streaming black-eyed
Archangel's silence
someone on his bronze horse I have seen before
leaps through snowfall,
moonfall, to the light,
willing me icons and a winter sea. ∎

FIRST SPRING DAY

It is

the first spring day.
I walk unsolved
through a child's primer
of the country,
fingers crossed,
for I am here and you are
maybe there
though not with me.

Shall I
pretend I cannot hear
the opening echoes of the year,
the noisy crocuses,
old children
courting merriment on the lawn?

Somewhere happiness
(days that we might spend)
hides. Half-believing
I could deny its end
by a child's magic, the romance
of will, the vow to ban
my ready jests, my pride

before your sunburned smile
(that lights the airport,
lights a world inside
when you come home cold public nights)
fades unbelieving,
instantly, away.   ■

SECOND DAY SPRING

It is

the second spring day
and all the flowers bloom
behind a black nag's ear
in Central Park.
Tanned lotharios of the street
call to me from their truck,
whistle from excavations as I
hurry by

on slim feet.
I smile and wave to them,
myself again,
for it is Rome and I am
radiant, twenty, fresh from luck,
your love, and once more
mistress of the dark.   ■

THIRD SPRING DAY

It is

the third spring day.
I run resolved
down suncaught rivers
in the country.
Grass is my shore.
I sit on Alexandra's swing
humming to hummingbirds
fashioning for percussion
subtle words

to fix the inconstant sun
at spring.   ■

Not to have learned
the name of the thing—

the yellowbarked tree
I climbed in sorrow,

the stones in the quarry
under the bridge

the preening reptile I startled,
the deer on the ridge,

the gray delicate bird
on marked wings gliding

swift as tomorrow
the terrain you stroll,

the trails of blue flowers I follow
from the edge of an afternoon

forest to the graveknoll,
your spring—

not to remember
the name for darkness:

not to escape
the time of a child

and never to find you
beyond the first place you smiled. ∎

Romancer, I write letters
that I never send,
to gambler and tree-surgeon,
cardinal and prophet,
a lover I still covet
as a friend.

You who married me
when the urns of child-scarred
stone were tall
ivy fountains, and patience
bloomed in the irongate garden,
and image was all,

could scarcely guess
how faithful, full of faith
for you I'd be.
Nor would I want you to.
Image is all.

Except today,
recognizing you
lengths ahead of me in Rome
strolling the venders' streets
we courted on,
Trastevere to Janiculum

your arm around her
(you, stronger than you'd been,
she, as I was then,
graceful and seventeen)
your world,

I wonder for a moment:
where is mine?
Your bare fine arm,
your eyes and wit like hers
were mine in Rome

that flowers forever
over the old grilled courtyards,
open windows full of arias,
soft sienna palaces
in the green clattering
of spring.

Shall I say,
look back and take my hand?
I want to hold you both wherever
you're going.

Shall I say,
I'm happy here, I'll stay,
flirting with peacocks in the
Villa Sciarra,
or will you ask me why,
and why we came?

I've forgotten, now.
I said it as a chant for two,
for three of us. How
many daughters?
"Why are you happy here?"

Those letters that you find
where I pretend
serenity, or palate for new
landscapes, gods, risks,
or a girl's romance,
I meant to send.

■

Whatever you may hear
I care.
Life is too wrung
with chimes and brass applause
for me to face,
though I would trade
the medals that I wear
for lace.

Whatever you may see
trust my despair.
Yesterday my love was caught
in a throat of fears
by tongues and ears
its own tide
beset.

Today
I tie a ribbon in my hair
and keep a diary of regret.   ■

MYOPIA

Being nearsighted has its rewards.
From my window, the tall
farmer squinting at sunset over his dry fall
wheatfields is you. The jaunty bill-
collector striding up Rucum Hill
humming through the morning mists
I welcome: you.

The secret tennis star smashing his serves
into the far court, who twists
to feminine applause (which he deserves)
as I arrive,
the blue-chip
man in the suit, alive
and rounding Fifth Avenue at a fast clip,
the sunturned scholar stretching among
admirers on the beach, my landing,
startles me (I knew it all along): you.

My fields blossom in December.
The world's lottery is mine to win.
My opponents are demolished in games
they won't even remember.
New York isn't dirty or boring,
airplanes and audiences don't scare me, adoring.
I'm a woman and this season I'm *in*.

Travel I shall, boldly by myself to Rome,
and watch you winding on a Vespa to church
from my perch
in a baroque dome.

I'll scan Feltrinelli's windows and each of
its posters, from across the street—
one, oh all of them announce, to be
performed nearby and soon, some feat
of yours. They've built a statue to you
high in Garibaldi Park
because you come there every day at dark
to praise Garibaldi and the view.
I'll be there, too.

Life quickens constantly for me.
I am ready noon and night
to draw my pen, my swords.
As long as I sense you near, Love,
being nearsighted has its rewards.   ■

A SUMMER'S LIE

No intimate of perfection, I honor these:

the flawed man
sick of his crimes
whose beauty is constant daring

the hunter of grizzlies
whose twilight eye
trembles for deer on the lawn

the glittering craftsman,
magician to millions, who,
polishing demon and doubt to gold,

smiles in their mirror
his heart cleft
by a single delicate spurning.

Not that I turn from
the blind man's dream, my
love's white clover that wakes the lawn

or the deep anemones
a child holds,
bouquets to redeem us all.

Only, I am at ease with the wild
tumbled grasses, the madness of swamps
and hurricane seas,

with the saltmarsh roses
whose brambles tear
my skin at the entrance to moors.

And I am friend to the soldier spinning
his summer lie,
caught, nearly through,

in the shining filaments that bind us
each to each other's protection.
I am the keeper of summer's lie

and would not spoil perfection.   ■

I walk through birches white and gray
over the graveyard's back
to catch the sun on an icy slate
etching a name by winter's light
I loved when this hill was golden, gay,
and the young deer left no track.

Perfect in snow, Connecticut
conceals each chasm and rock;
its charcoal branches draw the eye
upward from memory to sky,
but still my heart in slate is cut
and the river, still, is black.   ■

Suppose I weren't in love with you.
Think of all the good and true
men my fancy'd lead me to

        the one whose roving eye
        faultlessly searches
        the ocean floors
        the source of springs
        the reach of sky

        the one whose fine-tuned ear
        catches incredibly
        the lovesong of bees
        the nightsong of frogs
        the windsong meaning geese

        the one whose hands, dead-still
        move to the pulse
        of joy breaking in the rain
        of hope flirting the ravine
        of fear, the world's and mine.

Far down, alarms ring, noisily.
Suppose you weren't in love with me,
My Valentine.   ■

Strange that I can't remember
how you look.
I knew so well.
Pictures I encounter
in someone's book
may tell
me how you seem.

My eyes still feel
the blaze the altering
color of yours.
My lips my tongue seal
themselves around the sense
of yours.
The rest of me still watches
starts, races through the darks.
At the hint of spring
my heart catches
larks.

Still
unless you turn again
the appointed corner,
appear at my door,
its height and angle primed
for angels then
but man once more,
I cannot imagine who you are
or were before
the catalyst of dream.

We are committed to language,
we mutable birds,
denying that the constant cardinals'
songs reveal

that image is illusion,
loyalty, will—
desire, a reel.

We are committed to images;
cruces of words,
in the presence of witnesses
our intent conceal.

We are committed to loyalty
especially where
reason and other juries
find it absurd.

From the soul's sentence
there is no appeal.

And lately committed to desire
that spins us
higher than ever we meant
into the pure air

where sense is blurred
and after a space leaves us
to fall free, and heal.

I would commit the scarlet
countryside to song,
to leaving us,
we two, unheard,

language and the flight from it
our Catherine wheel.   ∎

My enemy
has golden hair
eyes of summer
mind as fair
as landscapes
on Peconic Bay
and worse:
he knows my way.

My enemy
is far too tall
alone in spring
in touch with fall
braver than I
too swift of stride
to wait for me.
What pride

devils and roots me
where I've been,
turns all my caring
outside in,
fathoms my passion,
feeds my will?
Enemy,
hold still.   ■

Love, there is no
scanning of the night
without you. Star and staccato
star interrupt the air
mock my soft tune
even as the wind, your wake
mocks the perfect
crystal of my reason.

The rising moon,
caught on your mast a moment,
barely a moment gone,
alters the rhythm of the swell
too fast,
cleaves every course I,
amateur of evening, chart.

Useless to surmise
I'll miss you any less
because I choose to sail
the bright, the brittle seas
of summer for a while
where you turn inland,
toward the dark.

Or to pretend I'll follow,
knowing your fears,
or seek the shadowed cove where
you must hide
from the green landfalls
of my vision.

Under the rain of willows, Love,
anchored to our pasts,
what time we'll mark.
Would that our graves were one,
the night not clear,
even, the concerto of our lies
about to start.   ∎

SASHIMI

After raw fish and conversation
my conclusion is
there aren't enough of us, John.

Selves may be forgot
for the season that we succeed,
though we continually fail,
but our intention
must not.

Integrity
born of direct affection,
as attraction, of recognition,
and our loyalty to truth

      meaning:
      loyalty
      to lightning
      no matter what ringed
      heart its striking
      may divide

      to bloodroot
      whose palest
      petals may belie
      its courage to grow
      by a slick
      highway
      or the singed
      alley (how the old
      woods burned!)

to the friend
who in hours of joy
would pick
you or me simply
as brother
even if his bravado
asks too much
of us now,
and tomorrow

crucifies the distance between
God and Satan
when days of our opportunity touch
us continually with sorrow.

Let us be true to one another
for the world which seems,
in whatever number.   ■

I had not lost to tenderness
since the days were trees.
Then in our vaulting treehouse
with leopards tamed below
we sang, green in a green
umbrella, and only sunlight
now and then spotted our purity.

I had not seen you, touched
the shadows in your face
since we climbed down,
nor felt my heart give way
under the force of the arrogant
game we wanderers play

till now, with the train's
lurch, it gives,
green though the train is gray
and going somewhere else.

How can I break
the years, the tracks of will?
Not knowing what I've
touched, you go
—blinded but oh, alive!—
to a frail town, a shrouded hill.

And I, unboned by memory,
away from poetry
and trees shall move again
toward the sun-baked
fortress where I live, am known.   ■

Star, be steadfast for a moment
after art.
The turning heavens you grace forever
this solstice night
won't start
without you.

Because I've shone
in the arc of your incandescence,
your close light,
I know:

faith is essence,
a sheltered hilly street we found
high in Carona.
Whoever you paused to touch
there, spying on your perfection
contracted gold.

The other evening
(it was unbearably cold
and you were streaking somewhere
far and lovelier away)

you let sparks fly.
Careless
perhaps, exposing
a piece of yourself to loss.

In such
accidental radiance
I saw you not quite whole
and, vulnerable,
more beautiful than ever.

Burying the sparks,
the piece you left, going,
I'm on my own
way to heaven now,
a different climb through all those darks.

Nothing can stop me.
But if for a flickering instant
you should find
too sharp

the firmament, the chilly
steepled, ever-demanding sky,
shine for me.
I aim to be
nearby.   ■

Anniversary.
Too many years to remember.
I dream
we are in Rome again, studying
the floppy orange guidebook,
lying on the brown bed
in the brown room
five steps down from the street.

Carlo knocks. Knocks.
Is it morning already? Noon?
Raining?
Is there a message? Someone
waiting? The voluptuous
lady over our heads
goes on with her tangled passion:
Sonno agitato.   ∎

The opportunity gone
the fault mine

I wake at gun-
point every dawn

I could have held you,
held you.

In this stretching
children's frieze of

order, beauty, home,
this many-handed game

I used to love,
look for the King.   ■

The air is nearer
        than it was in June.
Jade feathers scrape
        the gray silk sky
and all of Paris
        rustles:
it is September.
           Shy

girls with trailing ribbons,
        poets with sideburns,
lean on each
        precipice over the Seine.
Les Invalides takes a deep breath
        and praises mortality.
Notre Dame needles
        heaven again.

How many times
        I've stood on this balcony,
Dix Quai D'Orléans,
        and dreamed that we could stay
watching children
        in the Tuileries,
sailboats in Luxembourg Gardens,
        Montmartre, Monet.

More than enough, those dreams.
                But all the children
have grown wings, bloodied
                their beaks on stone,
their breasts on the sharp knives
                of their own vision.
To darker cities
                they have flown.

Good-bye, Paris. Shine as we leave
                each glistening
street, secret air,
                September,
and track them across the snows
                and oceans,
and, who knows?
                be part of their dream. Remember.   ■

Cheers! A new love,
late love back.

How intense the blue
above, how sharp the ice
and black.
How fair
the dappled hillside,
fierce the tide,
welcome the winds again.

This morning, spice
filters the air.
Tears
salt the fen.
The old familiar street
blossoms in strangeness
everywhere.

Tangles of fears
(your guess
isn't absurd: I missed
their company)
distract my feet.
Shall I say all I feel?

Only the night
is real
and honesty, that sweet
indulgence I would bear,
never comes right.

Still, a new
brilliance in me, blue
incredible delight
makes sense of the word.   ■

PROFILE

Lucifer, the intaglio
of your scarred sideturned face
carves every April branch I bend to,
luminous flower I rhyme,

burns on the uncut flyleaf
of the book I choose for night,
marring the smile of each new
child of grace
who dares to call my name.

I've promised not to touch you
though I marvel at the chime
of a tower you lift your lashes to,
a clock your fine hands trace,

only to spy where you bend
lighting, still,
a heart's unholy flame,
never to speak of spring, destroy you
turn, as fall, in your embrace.   ■

Somewhere the light is falling.
Yesterday sycamores
bent low to the River James,
a sweep of lawn, the blue-held air,
a long Virginia dream
that buoyed the morning.

Yet dawn is not so fair
on the River James as here,
the underside of clouds burning,
a clear elm in the savage wind's
embrace. This Puritan ground
is rocked toward light
each promise of your coming.

See how the autumn barn's caught fire,
cloudfire, the silhouette of swifts
in the chimney veils driven. A trace
of April skims the ground.
The slant of hayfields,
brazed petals, branches
catch your nearness. The fragrance
of a moment, and we're gone.

Everywhere light is falling
tangling the golden willow's skein.
The snake will shed his
skin at dusk, and leaves let go
forever, limb and polish.

Before us, the ravines of sun,
darkness
and arctic air
How delicate the landscape of desire
and fathomless
the shadows of despair.   ■

STUDIO

I watch you
as you sit across the desk
from me, far from me,
scoring the page with your pen.

You listen to childhood's music
(I want it to be mine)
and as you draw its faces
blacken them clean.

Expert cartoonist,
who brought so recently
my world to sense,
I wonder what you mean.

WINTER WAR

Snow armored
birch woods
march through
Connecticut,
cut through
crooked stone
walls to my door.

Snow turned
unicorns
lie on my
slant roof
point down
crystal horns
ready for war.

Shall I
standing safe
this side of
bubbled panes
warmed by a
birch fire
burning too slow

fling wide
the door's old
oak to the
sharper air
and charge
the winter world,
and let love go?

■

DUELS

Gentleness
is what I cannot forget
though I play the conspirator
to Satan's duel
though I suffer him
to inflict his realms of
pain for our brief sharp glory,

how there was
everything when you came
bearing gentleness:
light-years of grace,
the heart winding upriver
where snows
kept bellflowers blue for the sky.   ■

I love you as the world loves
      sunrise on a January
            morning in Connecticut:
      snow in the night
was true,

clear as heroes
      black hickories
            trace the hilly sky
      and every
artifice of day is new.

I love you as the world loves
      meridians climbing
            Tuscan vineyards;
      grapes shine on bronzeleaf
altars till the blue

nightingale and lizard bring
      orchids they hid
            in early spring,
      and olive gardens
prune the view.

I love you as I love the world
      in all its fire
            as sunset leaves
      the hills, the vines,
the sidewalk, world without hue:

in secret, since you stood with me
      before the world
            and such eternity
      as chooses lovers for each other
knew.   ■

Good-bye, strict shores!
The sea's upon me.
I am gone
into a wilderness of waves.
The sky showers
incessant minnows.
The mud nourishes
my seaweed shroud.
The water's breath
in my breathless space
blows green as the stems
of Queen Anne's lace,
sweet as the motion
of leaves, desire
that led me early here.

How swiftly the starry minnows
disappear.   ■

AIRPORT

Still at the locked gate
(have I forgotten
where I was going, what I knew,
that the hour was late?)
my hopes hover.

I feel the cold
glorious
towers of the Kremlin,
the first snow slanting on the Neva,
the porphyry
of Lenin's tomb.

In the grave distance loom
starred legends of Zagorsk in blue
and gold, icons,
dark funeral fires, sheer fountains
spiring to Peter's palace,
each myth made new.

At mass I hear the shimmering
choirs and bells of old
monasteries tolling,
at theater flute and balalaika,
eerie Uzbek horn.
I scent in the earliest markets

fresh bread and fresh
bouquets, our whispering
everywhere, saffron, broom.
I taste amber and champagne,
the ripe sweet melon
whispering would burst

and find (there is no forgiveness:
the gates are locked)
all the shaded secret
alleys of an autumn way,
arbors green and rust, ripest
for strolling
when I have turned away.   ■

I
I cannot conceive
the world again
no god am I
without you

the fire's gone
ashes and painted
eggs lie
on the floor

a china leopard
stares at the spot
you animated
last

no spring
blows by
or sunlight
shears the door.

II
The world again
conceives me
lilac or dogwood
takes the hill

azalea shatters
the woods,
the nearest
robin's nest comes blue

the leopard
under its copper tree
plays games with
sunlight still

another's hands
straighten the day.
A comic wind
blows through.   ∎

Light, loss.
The willow bends
still green in November
and raspberry vines bear
incredible sweetness
under the leaves of frost.

Choices of some sense abound
outside the polls:
fresh incense from autumn
fires, sheared hills,
soft openings in old stone walls,
the numberless gold sheaves

of promise. Dark rivers wind
down to the open harbor.
Our Fathers
found curious freedom
in choosing New England.   ∎

ASSASSIN [61]
For J.F.K.

The grass is green
the sky is blue
the earth is round

this is the day
our best beloved
lies underground.

All that we see
all that we know
our hearts deny

round is the earth
green is the grass
blue is the sky.

At Arlington
the caissons roll
through Lee's repose.

Restless
in unaccustomed black
past the white rows

of other soldiers
here they halt.
Only a fly

afterthought
of our season's pride
won't die

at the flag's fall
the drum's cease
the bugle's sound

slow and forever
leave him
to the live ground.

As we walk home
which of us trusts
the path he knows?

The earth may move,
the flowers are still,
no fair wind blows.   ■

GRAVE AT SAGAPONACK
For Deborah

Away with dreams.
The potato fields stretch fair
as desire, far as my faith
on the early honeysuckle wind.
Fine clouds erase the hermetic scribblings,
clear the slates of sky.
East and West my horizons.

Where the pillars of Strá
hold Tiepolo's blue and fanciful dome
Napoleon walked
by the River Brenta, resting from wars
and long Palladian dreams.
I scan the Atlantic Ocean.

A windmill spins.
The dunes descend and herons
call me to mark their grace.
The copper beech, crown of your realm
(the flat green world
I return to cherish)
gleams where summer grasses bend.

A white moth, muse
to the idle blades of steel, dances.
Stallions aroused whisper at the fence,
toss from their manes a shower of poppies
scarlet as the broom is yellow;
the high hills of Tarquinia
shed their Etruscan dreams.

From across the Sound
a whirl of dust
harries her grave.
Sunlight catches the empty window,
the pitch of eaves, the tiles,
the quiet, the mussed hair of a small
boy strong under the vines.

Wild roses stir
in their restless thorns.
Away with dreams! The hour is new,
quickened by life
involved by love
and the sun afire on the road.
Wait for me
in the endless mansions of morning.   ∎

Islands of Childhood

Some afternoon when the wind is blowing
belling out from Nantucket Sound
and autumn arbors bow with grapes
and oak leaves star the ground

I'll play for you my lute of roses
weave you love songs on my loom
while all the silences I've crafted
to betray me, bloom.   ∎

Lambert's Cove!
A private dune
white sand and silence
not yet noon

a single osprey
near her nest
nor she nor I
a host, a guest.

Empty, a skiff
waits where the grass
slants to smooth stones
and a looking glass

secret minnows,
buoys gone by,
island horizons,
endless sky.

Tomorrow's wind
blows from the west,
the fragile sea
shines in unrest

promising summer
long and soon.
Find me here
on the first of June.   ∎

MEMORIAL
For Van Wyck Brooks

A Bridgewater garden
the corner of town
a churchbell is tolling
the noon sun down

New England angels
in the dogwood sing
the white breath of sorrow
we hold this spring

A boy on a bicycle
stops by the tree
his face petaled white
under May's marquee

And smiles at us, quiet
on his corner lawn
till a breeze shakes the branch
and the shadow, gone.   ■

BULLFROGS

Bullfrogs strum
in the spring-rushed pond
fireflies lantern the willow
honeysuckle tangles
the lemon moon
and my feet dance a tempo
on the grass below
on the fresh damp grass
of our midnight pond
as they did when I was
—oh, thirteen—
and I forget
in this children's hollow
that I am grown
for the world's still green
and bullfrogs strum in tune.   ▪

The black rocks of Cuttyhunk
are diamond in the sun

The pale hills of Naushon
with sheep are overrun

Nonamesset, Pasque
and Nashawena gleam

beyond my sails in blue July,
the islands of a dream.

Some night in August
when harbors are asleep

I'll sail across to Naushon
and count the maze of sheep

and if, when startled cocks crow
the wind for home has died

I'll dig the deep blue mussels
from the morning tide.   ■

Lighthouse lady
tall and secure
white starched dress
and hat demure

watch for me
when the sun's gone under
beam me home
if there's fog or thunder

anchor my shore.   ■

Nantucket. Goblins of Ngorongoro
unhinge the night
as the mirage of days bent back
the wind, dense air.
A chill from primeval craters.
Wildebeest eyes
gleam in the dying windowfire.
Hyrax, hyena scream
where gulls cease to be.
Baobab uproots the cobbled garden
and black thorns shred each climb
to the holy spire.

Stars and I
walk a widow's walk,
haunting the sea,
inventing whaling days and promises:
dawn will come lavender
and very early. Oriental pearls
by noon will shine.
A tall mast on the sunset
horizon will be
looking for me.

AUGUST FOURTH

A mile and a half
    along South Beach
as far as my summer
    eye can reach
the sand is iced
    with colored shells
shiny as Easter
    hushed as bells

are hushed this morning.
    The island sleeps,
all but one
    who a calendar keeps
and, rising early,
    blows out the moon.
Someone is humming
    a birthday tune.

Falling asleep
on the beach in September,
the last ferry's oboe gone,
I am caught in the cobwebs
of dusk in the hammock
of wickets that sprouted
croquet on the lawn,
of lattices climbing
with trumpets and moonseed
and clouds in their halos
at dawn.   ∎

Good morning, gull,
my haven's guest.
Are you, like me,
riding unrest?

The shimmering tide
we float on now,
the downy sand
the full peach bough

like peace and I
belong to summer.
Gull, can you hear
the autumn drummer?

Susanna, filled with autumn airs
a-dance on stony walls
spilling her cartwheels down the lawn
in red wool waterfalls

shakes me from my lofty perch
with memories of being
seven, in an apple tree,
and all my future seeing . . .   ∎

COUSINS

Out at the Apple Farm my cousin and I,
freedom in the heart and devil in the eye,

hid from Nanny underneath the screen
of an old old chicken coop, flat on the green

grass—underneath the chicken coop just we two
of the Apple Farm had a summer's-end view;

an acorn, shiny on the drying grass,
waiting for the first fall squirrel to pass:

a row of chicken feed a boy would spill
hoping that a wild bird would eat his fill;

the farmer's shoes at the bottom of his tree
and a basket, empty at the farmer's knee

and a voice calling, "Children, where *are* you now?"
and children as quiet as the rusting plough

we could see way off where the clover ends
(cousins, conspirators, and just now friends!)—

a field mouse near us wriggling his nose,
listening for a signal a field mouse knows

and Nanny's voice sounding oh so cross
and smiles on our faces as we guess her loss

and the sun getting lower and the shadows long
and the oriole's slow twilit song,

the world suspended from light and sound,
the night unbidden, and we unfound!

And Nanny crying now—did we dream
such perfect fruit for our Sunday scheme?

the apples plucked, the field mouse gone,
silence everywhere, the long game won.

And all of a sudden our crying, too
for Nanny and the dark we were cousins to.　　■

Green freighted obelisk
leaning into blue

cypress on the mountain ledge
and Gandria my view

racks of rusted golden spools
sliding to the lake

brick chimney birdhouses
all my souls to take

and crates of rosy apricots
windowed in water's shine

if I should die before I sleep
this edge of heaven is mine.   ■

Flying fish and soaring kites,
leaping cliff and sliding sea,
race with me to Windy Gates
where summer hearts run free.

Midnight's broom has swept it clear,
no footprints blur the miles of sand.
Come, while I find (oh be there
still!) morning's old fantastic land

where elephants rest on tumbled clay
and lions yawn beyond the moor
and shiny hippos heave a sigh
as waves retrace their shore.

Once a long-lashed dolphin swam
in circles, blinked his eyes at me
and wounded, circling far from home
lay on the beach till I could see

no help or hope. I ran, crying
in vain, and, back, I knelt to feel
his chilly skin, his breath slowing,
his view that he and I were real.

Darting shorebird, dancing beast,
friend returned and child of tide,
race with me at Windy Gates
lest our hearts collide.

AFTERNOON SUN

Afternoon sun
on the laurel leaf willow
sloping to the edge of
Magog Lake

two white chairs
on the lawn's green pillow
far into dreams
my soul will take

bluest to the bells
as the monastery
peals a memory that
childhood sowed

and the mountain ash
still bright with berry
and the silvery porcupine
hunched on the road

Firefly or lantern
glows now above me
weather vane and constellation
turn with the fall

a friend is mine
sharing all that's lovely:
copper by the fire,
roses by the wall.   ∎

September, and the Shenandoah
fantasy of brigantines
sails to windward, grandly
down the real horizon points her prow

and disappears. In Vineyard Haven
we, bereft on docks and lawns
dream a last voyage, watch her go
taking summer with her, now.   ■

I knew they'd come
  the enormous yellow
    Norway maple leaves and green
      still tumbling into the pachysandra
        the fresh-piled smoky applewood logs
          glider we swung to tales of love on
        rusted wire encircling the well
      feathers and milkweed and alchemy's leaves
    whirling under the cold sun
  the last breath of our longest summer
down . . .   ■

My island in the morning
is the palest porcelain sky
a gull call and a whistle
and the ferry gliding by

clematis spilling on the hedge
and children on the pier
and sounds of summer everywhere
I turn again to hear.

My island in the morning
is blue enameled sky
clouds that hide a thousand kites
and sailboats slanting by

grasses to rouse my early feet
shells to rule the sands
and miles of crystal mirroring
the long-bright lands.

The flowered walks of Kitchener's way
feluccas on the Nile
a Chinese junk from Zanzibar
high temples in Tikal

and labyrinth and white fjord
volcano, cave, and cay
and spice routes to the Orient
set spinnakers for me.

My island in the morning
is a pomegranate sky
the bay a pewter symphony
as geese go honking by

mica panes that glisten
from the houses on the beach
a lighthouse like an Indian scout
measuring autumn's reach.

O island of my mourning
a foil and tissue sky
the echo of a foghorn,
an airplane silvering by,

a sea of opals breaking,
a moonshell opening wide,
and fishermen gone seeking
where the lucks of winter ride. . . .

Stay as the morning, island,
a changing song and sky
a lover, a deceiver
and my life goes skimming by

in stormclouds and a turning wind
fresh rain and spits of foam
the bay a sudden topaz
and a rowboat coming home.   ■

Softly the snow
falls from our sky

swiftly the geese
to green counties fly

honking their warning
to fair birds behind them

(where in the kingdom
of snow shall I find them?)

White birds in summer
shine by the sea

bright birds in autumn
jewel my tree

but now, brave as beauty,
old blackbird and crow

strut in this loneliness
knights of the snow.   ■